WHAT DO WE KNOW ABOUT
THE SOLAR SYSTEM?

Ian Graham

Chicago, Illinois

www.heinemannraintree.com
Visit our website to find out more information about Heinemann-Raintree books.

To order:
☎ Phone 888-454-2279

🖥 Visit www.heinemannraintree.com to browse our catalog and order online.

Edited by Andrew Farrow, Adam Miller and Adrian Vigliano
Designed by Marcus Bell
Original illustrations ©Capstone Global Library 2011
Illustrated by KJA-artists.com
Picture research by Hannah Taylor
Originated by Capstone Global Library Ltd.
Printed in China by South China Printing Company, Ltd.

15 14 13 12 11
10 9 8 7 6 5 4 3 2 1

Library of Congress Cataloging-in-Publication Data

Graham, Ian, 1953-
  What do we know about the solar system? / Ian Graham.
     p. cm.—(Earth, space, & beyond)
  Includes bibliographical references and index.
  ISBN 978-1-4109-4161-9 (hc)—ISBN 978-1-4109-4167-1 (pb) 1. Solar system. I. Title.
  QB501.G73 2012
  523.2—dc22   2010040166

Acknowledgments

The author and publishers are grateful to the following for permission to reproduce copyright material: Corbis pp. 14 (©epa/Dennis M. Sabangan), 19 (©NASA), 35 (©Roger Ressmeyer), 36 (©Mike Agliolo), 38 (©Charles O'Rear); NASA pp. 9, 11 (ESA/ CXC, JPL-Caltech, J. Hester and A. Loll (Arizona State Univ.), R. Gehrz (Univ. Minn.), and STScI), 12, 13, 15 (Goddard Space Flight Center Scientific Visualization Studio), 16, 18 (ESA/ I. de Pater, and M. Wong [UC Berkeley]), 20, 21 (JPL/ University of Arizona), 24, 28 (JPL), 29 (PIRL / University of Arizona), 31 top, 31 bot, 33, 37 (JPL), 39 (JPL/Cornell), 39 (JPL/ Cornell), 41; Science Photo Library pp. 4-5 (©NASA/ JPL), 6 (©Lynette Cook), 7 (©Take 27 Ltd.), 8 (©Gavin Kingcome), 10 (©Mark Garlick), 23 (©Mark Garlick), 25 (©John Sanford), 27 (©Paul Wootton), 26 (©Pekka Parvianinen), 30, 32 (©NASA), 34 (©Walter Pacholka, Astropics), 40 (©John Chumack); shutterstock p. 17 (©corepics).

Cover photograph of Earth and the Moon orbiting the Sun reproduced with permission of Science Photo Library (© Steve Munsinger).

We would like to thank Professor George W. Fraser for his invaluable help in the preparation of this book.
Every effort has been made to contact copyright holders of any material reproduced in this book. Any omissions will be rectified in subsequent printings if notice is given to the publisher.

Disclaimer
All the Internet addresses (URLs) given in this book were valid at the time of going to press. However, due to the dynamic nature of the Internet, some addresses may have changed, or sites may have changed or ceased to exist since publication. While the author and publisher regret any inconvenience this may cause readers, no responsibility for any such changes can be accepted by either the author or the publisher.

EARTH, SPACE, AND BEYOND

WHAT DO WE KNOW ABOUT THE SOLAR SYSTEM?

Contents

Some words are shown in bold, **like this**. You can find out what they mean by looking in the glossary. You can also look out for them in the "Word Station" box at the bottom of each page.

Our Solar System

We can see the stars in the night sky, and everyone knows something about the Earth, the Sun, and Earth's only **moon** (''the Moon''). But how much do we really know about the solar system?

The basics

The solar system is the Sun, the planets, their moons, and everything else that travels through space with them. We live on planet Earth, one of eight planets that orbits the Sun. Everything in the solar system is constantly in motion. The planets spin and orbit the Sun. Moons spin and orbit most of the planets. Numerous pieces of rock and ice of all sizes fly around the Sun, too.

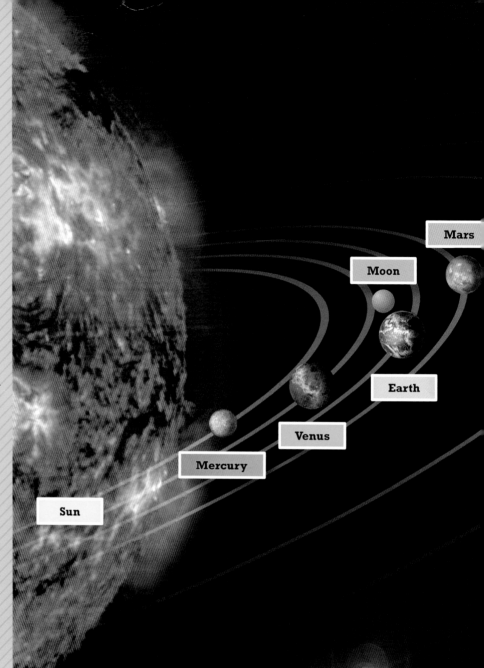

Mars

Moon

Earth

Venus

Mercury

Sun

Sun

The Sun is a star like many other stars in the sky. It looks bigger and brighter than the others because it is much closer to us.

Mercury

Mercury is the smallest of the solar system's planets. It is just over one third the size of Earth and just a little bigger than the Moon.

Venus

Venus is almost the same size as Earth, but its surface is permanently hidden under thick clouds.

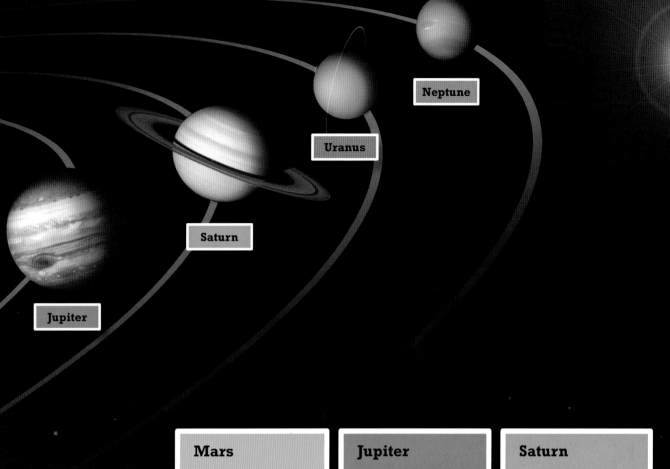

Neptune

Uranus

Saturn

Jupiter

Mars

Mars, called the "red planet," has seasons, polar ice caps, and a 24-hour day, like Earth.

Jupiter

The fifth planet from the Sun is the first of four giant gas planets and also the biggest planet in the solar system.

Saturn

Saturn looks like no other planet because of the beautiful rings that surround it.

Earth

Our home planet is unique. It is the only planet with liquid water on its surface and the only planet where life is known to exist.

The Moon

Earth's constant companion in space is the fifth-largest moon in the solar system. The Moon is about one-fourth of the size of Earth.

Uranus

Uranus was the first planet to be discovered since ancient times.

Neptune

Neptune is 30 times further from the Sun than Earth. It has the fastest winds in the solar system, with speeds of more than 2,000 kilometers per hour (1,243 miles per hour).

Where Did the Solar System Start?

The solar system was once a vast swirling cloud of gas and dust called a **nebula**. There was no Sun or planets. The Sun, the planets, their moons, and almost everything else that exists in the solar system today formed from this nebula.

A collapsing cloud

Nearly five billion years ago, the nebula began to collapse. The collapse may have been triggered by an exploding star. As the nebula fell in on itself, it started spinning faster. The spinning motion made the nebula flatten and become disc shaped.

Static electricity and the planets

Scientists made progress toward cracking the mystery of how the Sun and planets started forming in a 2003 experiment on the International Space Station. The question was: when the first particles bumped into each other, what made them stick together? Astronaut Donald Pettit brought scientists closer to solving the puzzle by shaking up grains of salt in a plastic bag. The grains immediately stuck to each other and formed bigger clumps held together by static electricity. Perhaps something similar happened in the **solar nebula** five billion years ago.

More than four billion years ago, the newly formed Sun was encircled by a dusty disc, where mountains of rock collided with each other, eventually forming the planets.

Particles of dust in the nebula bumped into each other. Some of them stuck together and formed bigger grains. Grains colliding with each other formed bigger clumps. These clumps swept up more and more matter, and grew bigger. The biggest ball of matter formed in the middle of the nebula. It became denser and hotter, eventually forming the Sun.

Clumps of particles flying around the young Sun formed boulders called **planetesimals**. Collisions between these formed bigger bodies called **protoplanets**. Eventually, collisions between the protoplanets formed the planets we see today. Planets near the Sun would have formed faster than the planets further away. Earth probably formed in about 100,000 years. Neptune, the furthest planet from the Sun, may have taken a billion years to form.

As the young Earth formed, it was bombarded by billions of boulders, which were flying around the solar system at that time.

You have weight because gravity pulls you down against the ground. Your mass is the same everywhere, but your weight depends on the strength of gravity.

The pull of gravity

Gravity is like an invisible glue that holds the solar system together. It keeps the planets in their orbits around the Sun. Gravity is a force that attracts one mass towards another mass. The bigger the mass, the stronger its pull of gravity. The Sun is by far the most massive object in the solar system. It contains 333,000 times more mass than Earth, so it has the strongest pull of gravity of any object in the solar system.

Up and down

Earth's gravity pulls everything towards the center of the planet. By pulling things down against the ground, gravity gives them weight. Gravity also tells us which way is up and which way is down. An astronaut floating inside a spaceship does not feel the pull of gravity, so there is no up or down.

Body matters

Our muscles and bones have to be strong enough to overcome gravity, so that we can stand up. Astronauts who go into space become weightless. Their body no longer feels the effect of gravity and it begins to change.

During a space flight, an astronaut's muscles become smaller and bones become weaker. Astronauts who go on very long space flights have to do at least two hours of exercise every day to slow down these changes. When they come back to Earth and feel the pull of gravity again, their muscles and bones slowly return to normal strength.

Quick weight loss tip: Move to the Moon

Your weight depends on the strength of gravity wherever you happen to be. The Moon's gravity is weaker than Earth's. If you traveled to the Moon, you would weigh one sixth as much as you do on Earth. Weaker gravity would let you jump higher, too.

bungee cord

Space station astronaut Nicole Stott exercises on a treadmill inside the International Space Station. Elastic bungee cords pull her down and help stop her from floating away.

What is the solar system made of?

The solar system is made of all the elements from hydrogen, the lightest and simplest element, to uranium, the heaviest element found in nature. Hydrogen and some helium were made by the Big Bang, the burst of energy that gave birth to the Universe about 13.5 billion years ago. But there were no heavy elements in the young Universe. These were made later by stars.

The largest stars die by blowing up in a huge explosion called a supernova. This sprays all the heavy elements a star has made into the surrounding space. In time, the dust and gas from these long-dead stars are swept up into giant clouds that form new stars and planets.

We are here because of stars that exploded billions of years ago. These stars threw the building materials for our solar system into space.

The Crab Nebula is a cloud of gas and dust thrown out by a supernova, or star explosion, in 1054 CE.

Are we unique?

We have no reason to think that our solar system is unique or special. If it formed in the way we think it did, we should be able to see other stars and planetary systems forming in the same way today. And we can. When astronomers look far beyond the solar system, they can see vast clouds of dust and gas where new stars are forming. And they can find young stars surrounded by dark dusty discs just like the disc of dust and gas that once formed the solar system's planets.

We are made of stardust

All the different elements that we are made of — including the calcium in our bones, the iron in our blood, and the carbon in all of our cells — were produced by stars. So, you can say that we are made of stardust. Stars also made the oxygen we breathe and the nitrogen that makes up most of the rest of the Earth's **atmosphere**.

Why does the Sun shine?

The Sun looks like a burning ball of gas, but it doesn't burn like a fire. Burning requires oxygen, but there is no oxygen in space, so something different makes the Sun shine. The mystery was solved in the 1930s. Instead of burning, the Sun changes mass directly into energy by a process called **nuclear fusion**.

An arc of glowing gas called a **prominence** hangs above the Sun's surface. Prominences can be hundreds of thousands of kilometers long and contain billions of tons of gas.

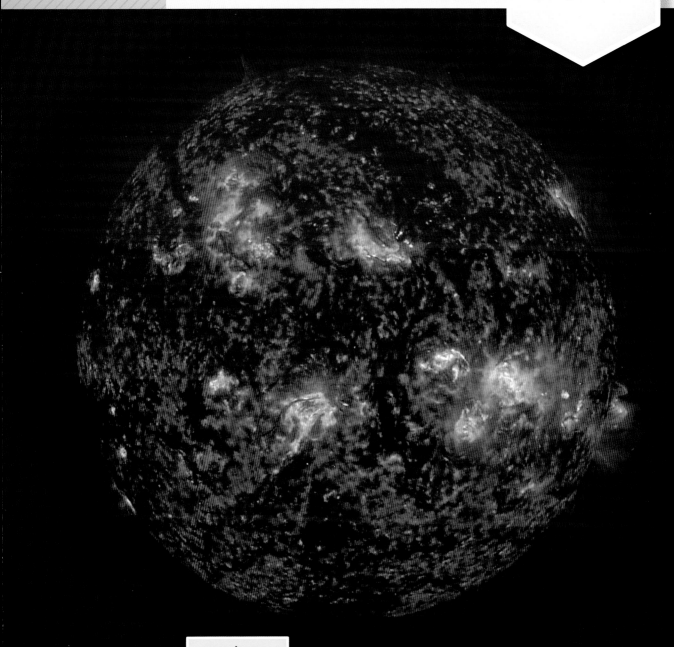

prominence

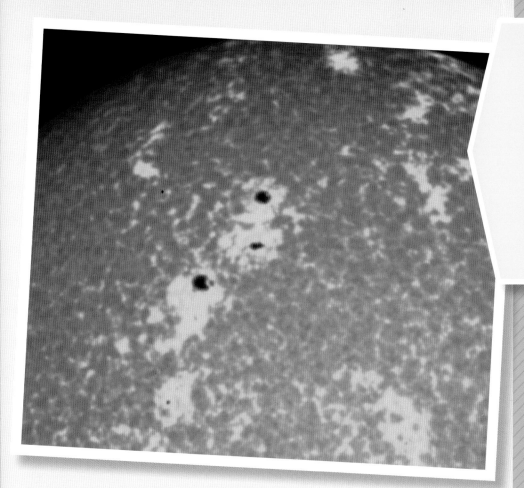

Light energy from the Sun's core takes years to travel to the Sun's surface, where it escapes into space. From there, it takes just 8 minutes and 20 seconds to cross 150 million kilometers (93 million miles) of space and arrive at the Earth.

The Sun is made mainly of hydrogen. The temperature in the center is about 15 million degrees Celsius (27 million Fahrenheit). At this temperature, hydrogen atoms are ripped apart, leaving their **nuclei** — the particles at the center of the atoms. Each hydrogen atom's nucleus contains a particle called a proton. The protons slam into each other and stick together, or fuse, forming a new element — helium — and giving out energy. So much mass is changed into energy in this way that four million metric tons of the Sun disappear every second. The Sun is so massive that it can continue losing mass at this rate for billions of years.

Two suns?

Jupiter is made of the same ingredients as the Sun (mainly hydrogen and helium). If Jupiter had become more dense, it might have become a star instead of a planet. Even though Jupiter is by far the biggest planet in the solar system, it would have to be about 80 times heavier to become a star.

What if the Sun were different?

If the Sun had been less massive or more massive than it is, the solar system would have formed in a different way. With a different mass, the Sun's gravity would have been stronger or weaker than it is. The planets would have formed in different orbits. In a different solar system, the Earth might have formed too close to the Sun, or too far away, for life to exist on its surface. With a different Sun, we probably would not be here.

The Family of Planets

The solar system's planets all formed from the same cloud of gas and dust, but they are very different worlds. There are two main types of planets — the small rocky inner planets and the giant gas planets in the outer reaches of the solar system.

What is inside a planet?

The ground we live on is a thin **crust** of rock that floats on the Earth's surface. Beneath the crust, there is a layer of denser, molten (liquid) rock called the **mantle**. It extends all the way down to the Earth's core. The core is a ball of metal, mainly iron with some nickel. The four inner planets – Mercury, Venus, Earth, and Mars – have similar core-mantle-crust structures. They are also known as terrestrial (Earth-like) planets.

The **gas giants** – Jupiter, Saturn, Uranus, and Neptune – are different from the terrestrial planets. Each gas giant has a small solid core surrounded by liquid and gas. Jupiter and Saturn are made mostly of hydrogen and helium. Uranus and Neptune also consist mostly of hydrogen and helium, but they contain water, ammonia, and methane as well.

How earthquakes help

We know what is inside the Earth because of earthquakes. Earthquakes send waves of energy through the Earth. The way the waves are bent and reflected, and the time it takes them to travel through the Earth, tells scientists what they have been traveling through.

Villages often thrive on the slopes of volcanoes, because the rich, black, volcanic soil around volcanoes is very fertile. However, these villages risk being wiped out by an eruption.

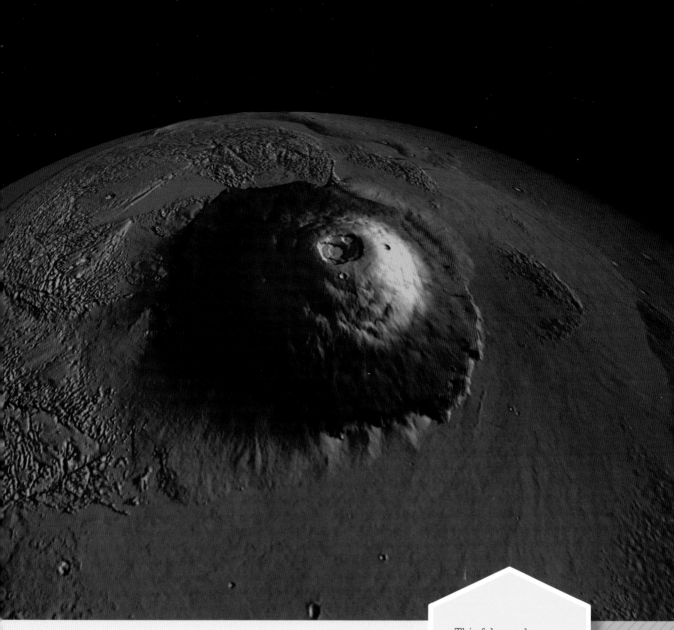

Plates in motion

The crust of rock that forms the surface of the Earth is different from the crusts of the other terrestrial planets. Earth's crust is cracked into seven major plates of rock and a dozen smaller ones. The plates move and their edges rub against each other. They often catch and get stuck. When they finally spring free, the result is an earthquake. In addition to this, molten rock melting its way up through the crust near the edges of the plates produces volcanoes.

This false-color image of Mars shows the biggest volcano in the solar system, Olympus Mons. It is nearly three times the height of Mount Everest, Earth's tallest mountain.

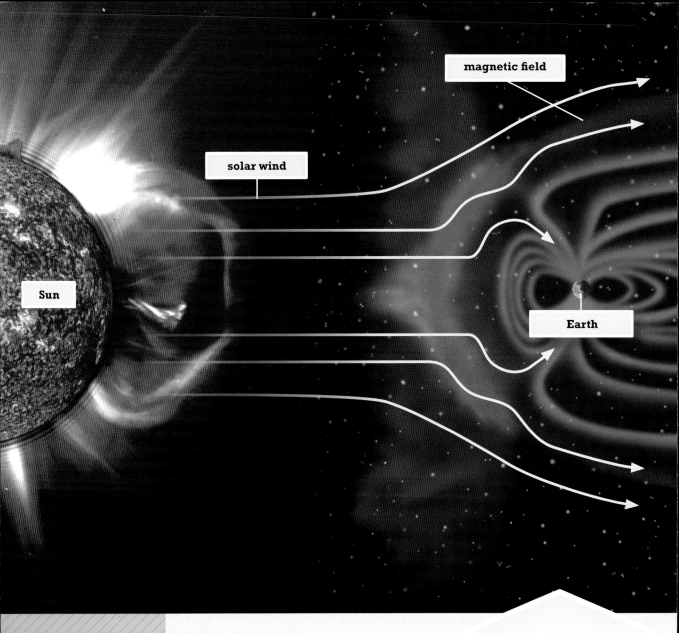

magnetic field

solar wind

Sun

Earth

Magnetic worlds

Planet Earth behaves like a magnet. Its magnetism is produced by its metal core. Not all planets are magnetic in the way that Earth is. Mercury has a weak magnetic field. Venus and Mars have no magnetic field, possibly because their liquid cores have cooled down and solidified. The gas giants — Jupiter, Saturn, Uranus, and Neptune — have strong magnetic fields.

Earth's magnetic field pushes much of the solar wind around the Earth and keeps it away from Earth's surface. The solar wind squashes the magnetic field on the Sun-facing side of the Earth and stretches it out into a long tail on the other side.

Lights in the sky

Particles stream out of the Sun in all directions at a speed of about 500 kilometers per second (310 miles per second). This constant outflow from the Sun is called the **solar wind**. Earth's magnetic field dominates a region of space, creating a protective shield that deflects solar wind particles around the planet. This region is called the magnetosphere. The shape of the magnetic field funnels the particles down into Earth's atmosphere near the north and south poles. When atoms of gas in the atmosphere are hit by solar wind particles, they give out light. Trillions of these collisions produce shimmering ribbons and sheets of glowing colors in the sky. This light display is called **aurora** borealis near the North Pole and aurora australis near the South Pole.

Aurorae (more than one aurora) don't just occur on Earth. They have been seen on other planets too. The Hubble Space Telescope has photographed aurorae on Jupiter and the Cassini spacecraft photographed them on Saturn.

The magnetic field

Earth's magnetic field helps us in two ways. It shields us from the solar wind, a stream of particles constantly being sent out in all directions by the Sun. It also enables us to find our way around by using a magnetic compass. Some animals, such as migrating birds, are thought to be able to find their way by sensing the Earth's magnetic field.

The sky over northern Canada is lit up by an aurora. Aurorae are caused by particles from the Sun plowing into the atmosphere.

Atmospheres

A planet's atmosphere is the mixture of gases that surround the planet. Mercury has almost no atmosphere at all. Venus has a very thick atmosphere. Earth has a thick atmosphere too, but not nearly as thick as Venus's. Mars has a very thin atmosphere. All of the gas giants have thick atmospheres.

The atmospheres of the planets are made of different gases. Earth's is mainly nitrogen and oxygen. Venus and Mars have mainly carbon dioxide atmospheres. The gas planets have atmospheres made mostly of hydrogen and helium.

Earth's atmosphere supplies the oxygen that we need. It also shields us from harmful radiation from the Sun and spreads the Sun's warmth around the planet. The weather we experience happens in the lowest layer of the Earth's atmosphere, called the troposphere. Other planets with atmospheres have weather too. On Earth, storms usually blow themselves out within a few days. On Jupiter, a storm big enough to swallow two or three Earths has been raging for hundreds of years. It was discovered by the English scientist, Robert Hooke, in 1664. It's called the Great Red Spot.

Jupiter's Great Red Spot is a giant storm. It rotates in a counterclockwise direction every six Earth-days. It has been spinning around Jupiter for hundreds of years.

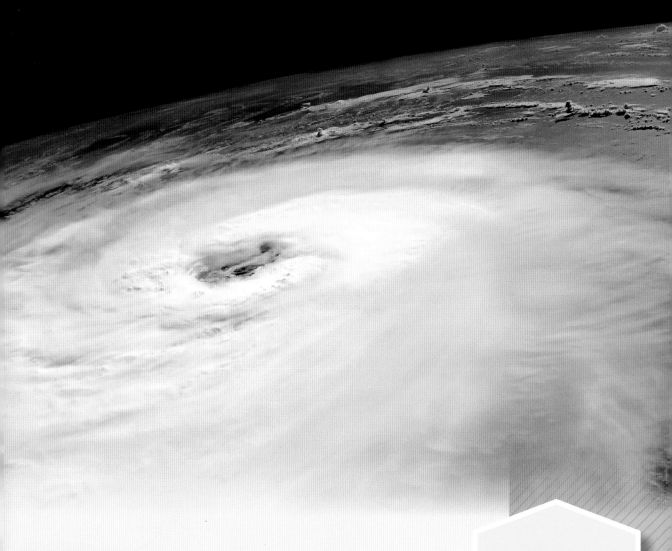

Moon gases

Moons are too small and their gravity is too weak to hold onto an atmosphere. However, there is one exception. Titan, a moon of Saturn, is the only moon in our solar system with a thick atmosphere. Scientists think its atmosphere is made of gas coming from inside the moon. The gas was trapped there when Titan formed and is slowly bubbling up to the surface.

The Sun's atmosphere

Stars have atmospheres too. The Sun's dazzling brightness normally makes it impossible to see its atmosphere. However, when the Sun is hidden behind the Moon, its atmosphere becomes visible. Like the Sun itself, the atmosphere is made mainly of hydrogen and helium.

A big hurricane or typhoon can easily be spotted from space, because it can measure more than 480 kilometers (300 miles) across.

Earth is mainly blue, because about 70 percent of its surface is covered with water. Water absorbs the red part of sunlight and scatters the blue part, which we see.

Why do the planets look so different from each other?

Earth looks like a blue ball hanging in the blackness of space. Venus looks whitish yellow, because of sunlight reflected by its thick atmosphere. Mars is red, because it is covered with a thin layer of dust that contains iron oxide, also known as rust! Mercury looks gray-brown, because that's the color of its bare, rocky surface.

Although the atmospheres of the gas giants are made mainly of hydrogen and helium, traces of other gases produce their different colors. Jupiter is red, orange, and white. Saturn is yellow. Uranus is blue-green. Neptune is blue. The planets look so different from each other, because their surfaces and atmospheres reflect different colors.

Jupiter's stripes

Jupiter is covered with bold stripes. They are bands of clouds produced by Jupiter's fast rotation and its distance from the Sun. Earth's atmosphere is very turbulent, because it is heated by the Sun. Jupiter receives only four percent of the solar energy that warms Earth. This makes Jupiter's atmosphere more stable, allowing the cloud bands to form and last a long time.

Rings

All four of the gas planets are encircled by rings. Jupiter, Uranus, and Neptune have thin dark dusty rings that are difficult to see. Saturn's rings are by far the biggest and brightest. They are so bright, because they are made almost entirely of ice, which reflects sunlight well. The rings are not solid. They are made of billions of pieces of rock and ice.

Probing Jupiter

One way that scientists find out more about planets is to send unmanned spacecraft to them to take photographs and gather information. When the Galileo spacecraft visited Jupiter in 1995, it dropped a mini-probe into Jupiter's atmosphere. The tiny probe found winds blowing at 530 kilometers per hour (330 miles per hour) while the Galileo spacecraft detected lightning flashes. The probe's instruments analyzed the atmosphere and found less water and helium than scientists were expecting. After only 57 minutes, the probe was destroyed by the immense heat and pressure of Jupiter's atmosphere.

Saturn looks different from all the other planets. This is because it is the only planet that is surrounded by discs of bright rings.

Orbit, Spin, and Tilt

It doesn't feel as if the Earth is moving at all, but it is actually moving very fast. All the planets move in two ways. They travel around the Sun and they spin. In addition, they tilt, or lean over.

Orbit

Earth travels around the Sun at a speed of about 108,000 kilometers per hour (67,100 miles per hour). If you could look down on the solar system from above the Earth's north pole, you would see the planets orbiting the Sun in a counterclockwise direction. They all move in this way, because the cloud the solar system formed from had a counterclockwise spin.

Earth takes 365.25 days to orbit the Sun, which gives us the length of our year. Planets closer to the Sun orbit faster. Mercury takes only 88 Earth-days to orbit the Sun. Planets further away orbit more slowly. Neptune, the furthest planet from the Sun, takes 165 Earth-years to orbit the Sun once.

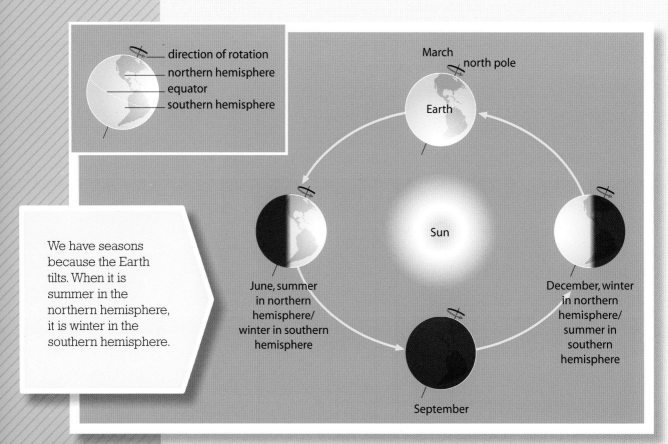

direction of rotation
northern hemisphere
equator
southern hemisphere

March
north pole
Earth

Sun

June, summer
in northern
hemisphere/
winter in southern
hemisphere

December, winter
in northern
hemisphere/
summer in
southern
hemisphere

September

We have seasons because the Earth tilts. When it is summer in the northern hemisphere, it is winter in the southern hemisphere.

The hazy blue-green planet, Uranus, tilts four times more than Earth. It lies on its side with one pole pointing at the Sun.

Spin and tilt

All the planets spin. Earth spins once approximately every 24 hours, giving us the length of a day. Someone standing on the equator is carried around by the Earth's spin at a speed of 1,670 kilometers per hour (1,038 miles per hour). When the planets formed, they spun in the same direction. Today, Venus spins in the opposite direction. Its spin might possibly have been reversed by a collision with one of the planet-sized bodies that roamed the early solar system.

All of the planets tilt, like toy spinning tops leaning over. Some tilt more than others. Earth has a 23.5-degree tilt. Uranus tilts so far that one of its poles faces the Sun!

Tilt and seasons

Earth's tilt produces the seasons. For part of the year, Earth's northern hemisphere tilts towards the Sun, bringing summer to countries north of the equator. As Earth continues on its journey around the Sun, the northern hemisphere tilts away from the Sun and cools down, heralding the arrival of fall and winter. It is the southern hemisphere's turn to tilt in the direction of the Sun and enjoy spring and summer.

When the Sun is blotted out during a total solar eclipse, darkness falls on the Earth, birds and animals fall silent, and the air cools.

A Sun-eating dragon?

Today, we know why solar eclipses happen, but in the past people did not understand why the Sun suddenly disappeared, turning day into night. A solar eclipse was feared. The word "eclipse" comes from a Greek word meaning abandonment, because the Sun seemed to have abandoned the Earth. Some cultures believed that a demon or dragon was trying to eat the Sun.

Eclipses

As the Moon orbits Earth and Earth orbits the Sun, the three bodies sometimes line up together. The result is an eclipse. There are two types of eclipse, solar and lunar.

A **solar eclipse** happens when the Moon passes between the Earth and Sun. The Moon is about 400 times smaller than the Sun. It is also about 400 times closer to us, so the Moon and Sun look the same size. When the Moon passes in front of the Sun, it casts a shadow on the Earth. The shadow has two parts, the umbra and penumbra. The umbra is the darkest part of the shadow. It is surrounded by a partial shadow, the penumbra. People inside the umbra see a total eclipse, the Sun disappears behind the Moon. People in the penumbra see a partial eclipse, the Moon passes in front of part of the Sun. The Sun looks as if someone has taken a bite out of it.

A **lunar eclipse** happens when the Moon moves into the Earth's shadow. Surprisingly, the Moon doesn't disappear. Earth's atmosphere bends sunlight around Earth and onto the Moon. Sunlight contains all the colors of the rainbow. The different colors in sunlight are made of light waves of different lengths. Blue light has the shortest waves, red light the longest waves. The waves that make blue light are exactly the right length to be scattered in all directions by gas molecules in the atmosphere. This is why a clear sky looks blue. The red part of sunlight, made of longer waves, travels through the atmosphere and onto the Moon, turning it red.

You might be lucky enough to see the Moon turning red as it passes into Earth's shadow during a lunar eclipse.

Moons and Their Effects

Moon rocks rock!

Several theories once existed to explain where the Moon came from. It might have formed next to Earth at the same time as Earth. It might have formed somewhere else in the solar system and was then captured by Earth. It might have formed after a collision between Earth and a planet-sized body. Scientists couldn't be sure which theory was correct until astronauts landed on the Moon and brought Moon-rocks back to Earth. The Moon-rocks were found to be identical to rock in Earth's surface, showing that the Moon must have formed out of rock that had been blasted into space from Earth after a collision.

A moon is a small world made of rock orbiting a larger body such as a planet. Mercury and Venus have no moons. Earth has one large moon, called the Moon. Mars has two tiny moons, called Phobos and Deimos. The four giant gas planets have dozens of moons.

Making moons

Most moons were chunks of rock wandering through the solar system until they were captured by the planets they now orbit. Earth's Moon is different. At first, Earth had no moon. Then, about 4.45 billion years ago, a planetesimal the size of Mars collided with Earth and blasted parts of both objects out into space. All the bits and pieces eventually collected together and formed the Moon. The planetesimal that collided with Earth was destroyed by the impact.

Changing shapes

The same side of the Moon always faces Earth, but the part we can see changes shape from night to night. We see more of the Moon's sunlit half every night until we see the whole sunlit half. This is the full Moon. Then we see less and less of it every night until it disappears altogether. This is the new Moon. These different shapes are called the phases of the Moon.

Changes in the shape of the Moon from night to night are caused by the changing positions of the Earth and Moon as they travel around the Sun.

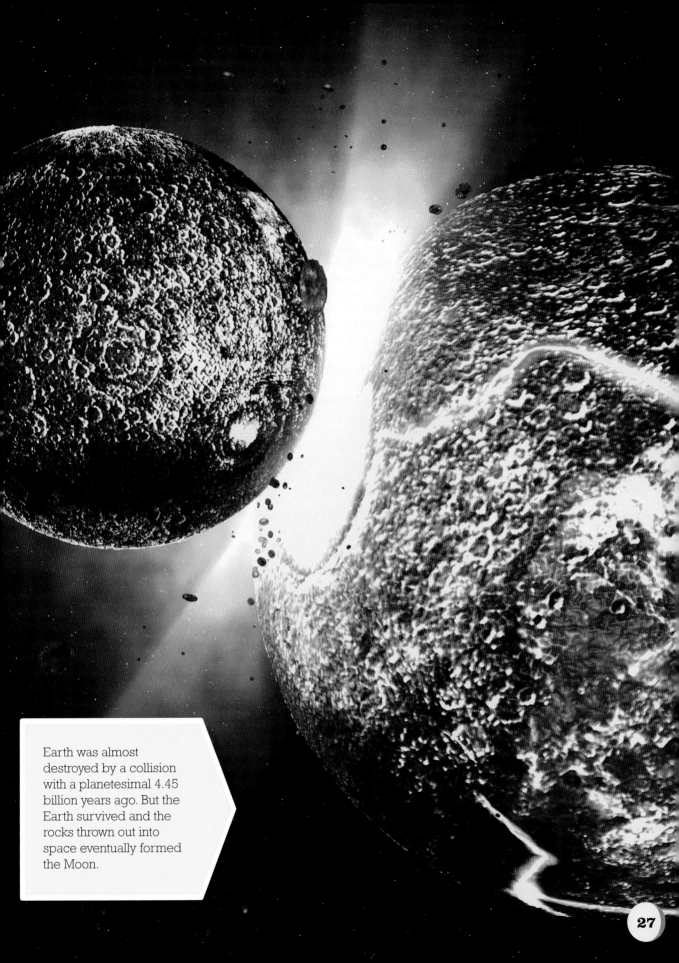

Earth was almost destroyed by a collision with a planetesimal 4.45 billion years ago. But the Earth survived and the rocks thrown out into space eventually formed the Moon.

What do moons do?

Moons are tiny compared to the planets they orbit, but they sometimes have important effects on the planets. The Moon affects Earth in one way that is very observable. Twice a day, the ocean washes up higher onto the shore and then falls back again. The two high tides that happen every day are caused by the Moon.

The Moon's gravity pulls the ocean toward it. A swollen bulge of water piles up on the Moon's side of Earth. A smaller bulge of water is left behind on the opposite side of the Earth. As the Earth spins, the two bulges try to stay in line with the Moon. The sea level rises as each bulge of water sweeps past and then falls again. High tides create deeper water for ships to sail in and out of ports. Low tides uncover lots of wet sand for children to build sandcastles on and lots of tiny creatures for birds to feed on.

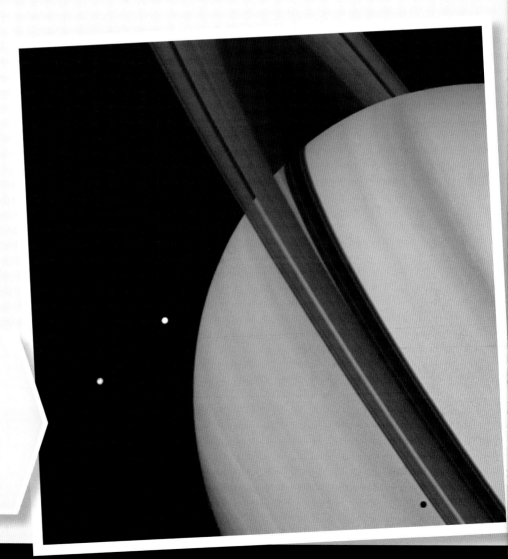

The gaps in Saturn's rings were caused by moons called "shepherd moons." The moons' gravity changes the orbits of particles in the rings, clearing the gaps.

Volcanic Io

Planets also affect moons. One of the most dramatic effects is seen on one of Jupiter's moons, Io. Jupiter's powerful gravity pulls and squashes Io as it orbits Jupiter. This produces hundreds of volcanoes that spew brightly colored sulfur onto Io's surface.

The Galileo space probe took this photograph of Jupiter's moon, Io, in 1999. The black, brown, green, orange, and red spots on its surface are enhanced false-colors to mark the locations of volcanoes.

Discovering the Solar System

The word "planet" comes from a Greek word meaning "wanderer," because the planets wander against the backdrop of the stars, which stay in the same positions. The first six planets (Mercury to Saturn) were known to astronomers in the ancient world, because they can be seen with the naked eye. The rest of the planets were not discovered until the telescope was invented.

Downsizing Pluto

In 2005, news reports announced the discovery of the solar system's tenth planet. It was named Eris. With this finding, and the previous discovery of two similar bodies, astronomers had to decide whether to call them all planets or keep the name "planet" for a few special bodies. In the end, they decided that Eris and similar objects would be called "dwarf planets." So, the solar system didn't have a tenth planet after all. Pluto, a planet until then, was reclassified as a dwarf planet. The number of planets in the solar system is now said to be eight, instead of nine.

In 1609, the Italian astronomer Galileo Galilei was one of the first people to look at the night sky through a telescope.

Hunting planets

In 1781, the astronomer Sir William Herschel turned his new telescope to the sky. He noticed a speck of light moving strangely. At first, he thought it was a **comet**. However, when its orbit was calculated, it turned out to be a planet. It was named Uranus after the ancient Roman god of the sky.

Astronomers found that Uranus was not moving exactly as they thought it should. They wondered if another planet could be tugging Uranus out of position. Mathematicians worked out where the new planet should be. In 1846, astronomers found it. This planet was named Neptune after the Roman god of the sea.

Finding Pluto

The solar system's ninth planet, Pluto, was discovered in 1930 by Clyde Tombaugh. It took him over a year of studying photographs to find it. The new planet was named Pluto after the ancient Greek god of the underworld.

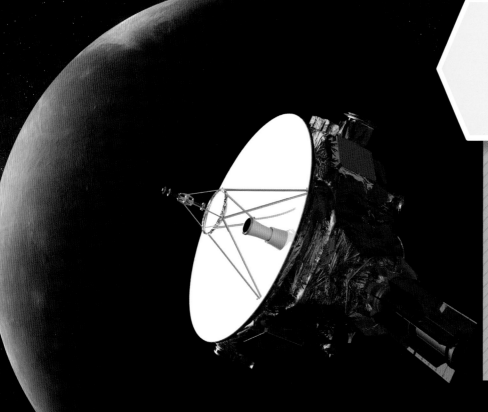

NASA's New Horizons space probe was launched in 2006 on the first mission to Pluto. It will arrive in 2015.

Looking for life

There is life almost everywhere we look on Earth, but what about the rest of the solar system? Life on Earth needs two things, energy and water. Water is plentiful on Earth and energy is supplied by the Sun. Planets closer to the Sun are too hot for liquid water and planets further away are too cold. Life was thought to be possible within a narrow band of space around the Sun called the **habitable zone**. The habitable zone is also called the Goldilocks zone, because planets within it are not too hot and not too cold – they're just right.

In the news

Are Martians worms?

On August 6, 1996, a **meteorite** from Mars called ALH84001 made front-page news all over the world. Some scientists who studied it found worm-like shapes inside the rock. They thought these might be signs of life from Mars. However, since then other scientists have shown that the "worms" are not related to life on Mars. It seems that life on Mars had not been discovered after all.

Could these worm-like shapes be the remains of organisms that once lived on Mars? Most scientists now think that the shapes are not evidence of life on Mars.

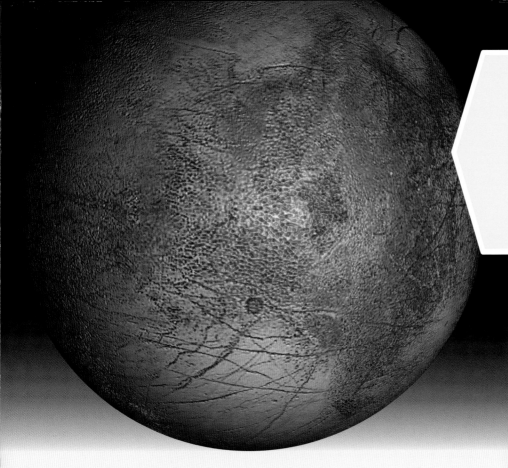

Jupiter's moon, Europa, has an icy surface that may cover an ocean of water. Wherever there is water on Earth, there is life, so there may be life on Europa too.

Where are the Martians?

In the past, some people thought intelligent creatures lived on Mars, but when space probes visited Mars they found no Martians. Mars is a dry, dusty world today, but water did flow on its surface in the past. Since then, some has evaporated into space, but life could have developed on Mars when water was plentiful.

Extreme life

When scientists explored the ocean floor in the 1970s they expected it to be lifeless, because sunlight never reaches it. They were amazed to discover towers of rock covered with snails, crabs, giant worms, and other creatures. The question was, without sunlight, where did their energy come from?

The creatures crowd around hot springs coming from beneath the ocean floor. Bacteria (microscopic organisms) obtain energy from chemicals dissolved in the water. These bacteria and other microbes are the base of the food chain there. If life can flourish in a place like that, maybe it could flourish in other parts of the solar system, even outside the habitable zone.

Space Rocks

As the solar system formed, billions of pieces of rock and ice did not become part of the Sun, planets, or moons. Many of them are still flying around the solar system today.

Hale-Bopp was the brightest comet of the 1990s. It's called Hale-Bopp, because astronomers Alan Hale and Thomas Bopp discovered it.

Photographs of Halley's Comet, taken by the Giotto space probe in 1986, showed a huge mountain of dark dust and ice 16 kilometers (10 miles) long.

Halley's Comet

Until 1986, no one knew if a comet really was made of rock and ice. As Halley's Comet neared the Sun in 1986, the European Space Agency sent a space probe called Giotto to meet it. Giotto flew through Halley's coma, the cloud of gas and dust around a comet. It photographed the nucleus, the solid part of a comet, from a distance of only 596 kilometers (370 miles). The photographs showed that comets are indeed made of rock and ice.

A comet is a mountain of rock and ice flying through space. Billions of comets circle the solar system in a region called the Oort Cloud. Collisions between comets or a tug from the gravity of a passing star can send a comet flying closer to the Sun.

As a comet nears the Sun, it warms up. Some of its ice changes to gas. Gas and dust coming off a comet stretch out into two long tails, a gas tail and a dust tail. The dust tail is bright, because it reflects sunlight. Most comets can only be seen clearly by looking at them through a telescope. Every ten years or so a comet big enough and bright enough to be seen with the naked eye appears in the sky.

Some comets have orbits that bring them back to our part of the solar system again and again. One of these, Halley's Comet, comes back every 76 years.

Points of light

The word "**asteroid**" means star-like, because asteroids were once thought to look like stars. They are actually pieces of rock. They are also known as minor planets or planetoids, because they orbit the Sun like planets. Most asteroids are less than 1.6 kilometers (1 mile) across. Nearly all of them are found in a broad band between the orbits of Mars and Jupiter, called the **asteroid belt**.

Asteroid collision?

From time to time an asteroid passes close to Earth. In the distant past, asteroids have actually hit Earth. One that hit Earth 65 million years ago may have helped end the age of the dinosaurs. If a large asteroid were to hit Earth today, humans might not survive. However, it is extremely unlikely that an asteroid will collide with Earth in our lifetime.

If a huge asteroid ever hits Earth, it might look something like this. Several organizations scan the skies, searching for any asteroid or comet that might collide with Earth.

Asteroid Ida has its own tiny moon, called Dactyl. Ida is 55 kilometers (34 miles) long. Dactyl is about 1.5 kilometers (1 mile) across.

Dactyl

Ida

Some asteroids are big enough to have their own moons. When the Galileo space probe traveled through the asteroid belt on its way to Jupiter in 1993, it photographed an asteroid called Ida. The photographs revealed a tiny moon orbiting it.

Where did they come from?

In the early solar system, the asteroid belt contained many large pieces of rock. They failed to come together to form a planet, because of Jupiter. Jupiter's gravity pulled on the rocks and caused many violent collisions between them, which broke up the rocks to form the billions of asteroids that we see today.

WORD STATION
asteroid body of rock bigger than about 10 meters (33 feet) across, found mainly in the asteroid belt

What is a shooting star?

Space rocks smaller than 10 meters (33 feet) across are called **meteoroids**. If a meteoroid as small as a grain of sand flies into Earth's atmosphere, it heats up so quickly that it glows for a fraction of a second before it burns up completely. It makes a streak of light called a **meteor**. Meteors are also known as shooting stars. When Earth passes through a trail of particles left behind by a passing comet, the result can be a great display of shooting stars called a **meteor shower**.

A meteoroid that is big enough to fly all the way through the atmosphere and land on the ground is called a meteorite. Scientists collect meteorites because they are very old pieces of rock left over from the formation of the planets and moons. They contain information about the early solar system.

This 1,200-meter (3,940-foot) crater in Arizona was made about 50,000 years ago by a meteorite 45 meters (150 feet) across and weighing 300,000 tons.

Meteorites on Mars

In 2005, newspapers announced that a robot called Opportunity had discovered a rock on Mars that might be a meteorite. It was named the **Heat Shield** Rock, because it was found near Opportunity's discarded heat shield. Tests show that it is indeed a metallic meteorite.

The basketball-sized Heat Shield Rock, discovered on Mars, was the first meteorite ever to be found on another planet.

Did meteorites start life on Earth?

Some meteorites contain chemical compounds called amino acids. These are the building blocks of life. More than 70 different amino acids have been found in meteorites. It is possible that life on Earth sprang from chemical compounds that were brought to Earth by meteorites.

A large meteorite makes a hole in the ground called a crater. The Moon is covered with craters caused by billions of years of meteorite impacts. There are few craters to see on Earth, because wind and rain wear them away and vegetation covers them.

Mars rocks

When the Moon and other planets are hit by meteorites, the impacts are sometimes so powerful that they send rock flying out of the surface all the way into space. A few of these rocks from the Moon and Mars have landed on Earth.

WORD STATION
meteor streak of light caused by a meteoroid entering Earth's atmosphere and heating up so much it vaporizes

39

Looking into the Future

The moving Moon

How do we know for sure that the Moon is moving 3.8 centimeters (1.5 inches) further away from Earth every year? Thanks to reflectors left on the Moon by the Apollo astronauts. Astronomers on Earth fire a **laser** at the reflectors, which bounce the light back to Earth. The precise distance between the Earth and the Moon can be calculated from the time the light takes to travel to the Moon and back.

The solar system will not last forever, because the Sun will not last forever. A few billion years from now, the Sun will run out of hydrogen fuel and begin a dramatic change.

The dying Sun will grow bigger and turn red, changing into a star called a red giant. It will swallow Mercury and Venus. Our home planet will probably spiral into the Sun and be vaporized too. Then the Sun will shrink and become a tiny cool star called a white dwarf.

A lifeless Earth

Long before the Sun changes into a red giant, most life on Earth will become impossible. The Moon is moving further away from Earth. Within 2 billion years, the Moon will be so far away that it will no longer steady Earth's tilt. Earth will wobble so much as it spins that most of the life on Earth will end.

Aldebaran is a red giant star about 65 light-years away in the constellation of Taurus. The Sun will change into one of these red giants a few billion years from now.

Earth's hot core is cooling down. When the liquid part of the core cools down enough to solidify, it will no longer produce a magnetic field. When Earth's magnetic field disappears, the solar wind will be able to sweep our precious atmosphere away into space.

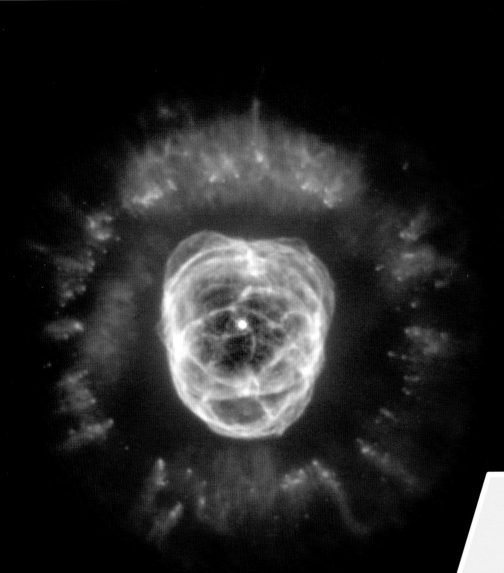

Starting over

Long after life on Earth has disappeared, the red giant Sun will push its outer layers away into space. The atoms that we are made of will become part of the Sun. They will be spread into space and may be swept up by a new star and planets forming somewhere else in space.

The Eskimo Nebula was once a star like the Sun. As it died, it threw off its outer layers, as the Sun will do, forming the complex patterns that surround it.

Timeline of Space Exploration Missions

Date	Mission	Description
1950s		
Oct. 4, 1957	Sputnik 1	first artificial satellite to go into orbit around Earth
Jan. 2, 1959	Luna 1	first spacecraft to fly past the Moon
Oct. 7, 1959	Luna 3	took the first photographs of the far side of the Moon
1960s		
Apr. 12, 1961	Vostok 1	carried Yuri Gagarin, the first man to orbit Earth
Aug. 27, 1962	Mariner 2	first successful interplanetary space probe – flew past Venus
Nov. 28, 1964	Mariner 4	first spacecraft to fly past Mars
Jan. 31, 1966	Luna 9	first lunar lander
Dec. 21, 1968	Apollo 8	first manned spacecraft to orbit the Moon
July 20, 1969	Apollo 11	first manned landing on the Moon
1970s		
Sept. 12, 1970	Luna 16	first robotic sample return from the Moon
Nov. 10, 1970	Luna 17	first unmanned lunar rover explores the Moon
May 19, 1971	Mars 2	first spacecraft to land on Mars
May 30, 1971	Mariner 9	first spacecraft to orbit another planet (Mars)
Mar. 2, 1972	Pioneer 10	first spacecraft to fly past Jupiter
Apr. 5, 1973	Pioneer 11	first spacecraft to fly past Saturn
Nov. 3, 1973	Mariner 10	first spacecraft to fly past Mercury
June 8, 1975	Venera 9	first pictures from the surface of Venus
Aug. 20, 1977	Voyager 2	flew past Jupiter and Saturn, and also first spacecraft to fly past Uranus and Neptune
Sept. 5, 1977	Voyager 1	flew past Jupiter and Saturn
Aug. 12, 1978	ISEE-3	studied the effect of the solar wind on Earth's magnetic field, and the first spacecraft to fly past a comet (Giacobini-Zinner)
1980s		
Apr. 12, 1981	Columbia	first launch of the U.S. space shuttle
Jan. 25, 1983	IRAS	launch of the Infrared Astronomical Satellite, the first spacecraft to photograph the whole sky at infrared wavelengths
July 2, 1985	Giotto	flew past Halley's Comet
Oct. 18, 1989	Galileo	first asteroid fly-by, first asteroid moon discovery, first Jupiter atmospheric probe and first fly-by of Jupiter's largest moons
Nov. 18, 1989	COBE	launch of the Cosmic Background Explorer, which discovered radiation left over from the Big Bang
1990s		
Apr. 24, 1990	Hubble Space Telescope	orbital space telescope
Dec. 2, 1995	SOHO	launch of the Solar and Heliospheric Observatory (SOHO) to study the Sun and space weather
Feb. 17, 1996	NEAR	first spacecraft to fly past a near-Earth asteroid, orbit a near-Earth asteroid (Eros), and land on it

Date	Mission	Description
Dec. 4, 1996	Mars pathfinder	landed the first rover vehicle, called Sojourner, on Mars
Oct. 15, 1997	Cassini-Huygens	first spacecraft to orbit Saturn, also landed a small probe on Titan, one of Saturn's moons
Nov. 20, 1998	International Space Station	launch of the first part of the International Space Station
Feb. 7, 1999	Stardust	first spacecraft to collect dust from a comet's coma and bring it back to Earth
2000s		
Aug. 8, 2001	Genesis	first spacecraft to collect particles of the solar wind and bring them back to Earth
June 10, 2003 July 7, 2003	Spirit and Opportunity	rover vehicles that arrived on Mars in 2004 and were intended to last three months, but were still working in 2010, although Spirit became stuck in soft soil in 2009
Mar. 2, 2004	Rosetta	due to rendezvous with comet Churyumov-Gerasimenko in 2014, Rosetta will orbit the comet and put a lander on it
Jan. 12, 2005	Deep Impact	sent a small impactor to collide with comet 9P/Tempel 1 so that the material kicked out into space can be analyzed
Jan. 19, 2006	New Horizons	will be first spacecraft to do close-up study of Pluto, due to reach Pluto in 2015

Planets – the Vital Statistics

	Distance from Sun	Diameter	Number of moons	Length of day (sunrise to sunrise)
Mercury	58 million km	4,880 km	0	176 Earth-days
Venus	108 million km	12,104 km	0	117 Earth-days
Earth	150 million km	12,756 km	1	24 hours
Mars	228 million km	6,794 km	2	24.6 hours
Jupiter	779 million km	143,000 km	63	9.8 hours
Saturn	1.4 billion km	120,000 km	60*	10.2 hours
Uranus	2.9 billion km	51,120 km	27	17.2 hours
Neptune	4.5 billion km	49,530 km	13	16.1 hours

More moons are still being discovered around the gas giants. By the year 2000, only 18 of Jupiter's moons were known. By 2003, more than 40 more had been discovered. More are likely to be discovered in future.

*The exact number of Saturn's moons is unclear but it is usually listed as at least 60.

Find Out More

Books

Couper, Heather, and Nigel Henbest. *DK Encyclopedia of Space.* New York, NY: DK Publishing, 2009.

Farndon, John. *Exploring the Solar System.* Chicago, IL: Heinemann Library, 2008.

Grego, Peter. *Discovering the Solar System.* North Mankato, MN: QEB Publishing, 2007.

Harris, Joseph. *Space Exploration: Impact of Science and Technology.* Pleasantville, NY: Gareth Stevens Publishing, 2010.

Jefferis, David. *Space Probes: Exploring Beyond Earth.* New York, NY: Crabtree Publishing Company, 2009.

Stott, Carole. *Space Exploration.* New York, NY: Dorling Kindersley, 2010.

Trammel, Howard K. *The Solar System.* New York, NY: Children's Press, 2010.

Websites

http://sse.jpl.nasa.gov/kids/index.cfm
Fun things to read and do from the U.S. space agency NASA.

http://athena.cornell.edu/kids/rover_human.html
See how you compare to a Mars rover.

http://spaceplace.jpl.nasa.gov/en/kids/mars_rocket.shtml
Go on a mission to Mars.

http://solarsystem.jpl.nasa.gov/planets/index.cfm
Find out more about the planets and their moons.

www.esa.int/esaKIDSen/LifeinSpace.html
Find out more about space exploration and life in space.

Places to visit

Smithsonian National Air and Space Museum, Washington, DC.
http://www.nasm.si.edu/

Kennedy Space Center, Orlando, FL, the nation's most comprehensive museum of space.
http://www.kennedyspacecenter.com/visit-us.aspx

Topics to investigate

Extraterrestrial life

Life may have developed on other planets or moons differently from life on Earth. What might life on other planets or moons look like?

Making Mars more like Earth

Humans cannot live on Mars as it is today. It's too cold, the atmosphere is too thin, and there is not enough oxygen in the atmosphere. Some scientists think Mars could be transformed into an Earth-like planet by a process called terraforming. How might you make Mars warmer and change its atmosphere so that humans could live on Mars without wearing spacesuits?

Asteroid approaching

If astronomers discovered an asteroid or comet heading for Earth several years before a deadly collision, how might its course be changed so that it misses Earth? Could it be destroyed or pushed out of the way somehow? The U.S. space agency NASA keeps a list of space objects that might be a danger to Earth. You can see the list at **http://neo.jpl.nasa.gov/risk**. The colors on the list show how dangerous each object is. If you find details colored red, the maximum danger, watch out!

The cost of exploration

Is the exploration of the solar system worth the cost? It costs millions of dollars to send a space probe to visit a planet. Manned space exploration costs billions of dollars.

Space weather

The changing conditions in space near Earth are known as space weather. The weather in space can affect satellites and manned spacecraft orbiting Earth. Electronic systems in spacecraft can be damaged and astronauts' lives may be at risk.

Glossary

asteroid body made of rock bigger than about 10 meters (33 feet) across found mainly in the asteroid belt

asteroid belt wide band of asteroids between the orbits of Mars and Jupiter, where most of the solar system's asteroids are found

atmosphere mixture of gases that surround a planet

aurora glowing, colored light in the sky caused by particles from the Sun colliding with gas in the atmosphere near the Earth's poles

comet ball of rock and ice that develops a bright tail or tails when it comes closer to the Sun than Jupiter

crust planet's outermost layer of rock

gas giant one of the solar system's four outer planets, Jupiter, Saturn, Uranus, and Neptune

gravity force that attracts masses towards each other. Gravity holds the solar system together.

habitable zone region of space where an Earth-like planet can have liquid water on its surface and life can exist

heat shield heat-resistant cover on a spacecraft that protects the craft from high temperatures as it enters an atmosphere from space

laser device that produces an intense beam of pure light

lunar eclipse darkening of the Moon caused when the Moon travels through the Earth's shadow

mantle molten rock layer of a terrestrial planet that lies between its core and its crust

meteor streak of light seen in the night sky, caused by a meteoroid entering the Earth's atmosphere and heating up so much that it is vaporized. Also called a shooting star.

meteorite meteoroid that enters the atmosphere from space and survives its fall all the way down to the ground

meteoroid piece of rock up to about 10 meters (33 feet) across traveling through space in orbit around the Sun

meteor shower large number of meteors seen when the Earth travels through dust left behind by a comet

moon small natural body made of rock orbiting a planet. Moons are also called natural satellites. Earth's only natural satellite is known as the Moon (with a capital "M").

nebula cloud of dust and gas, mainly hydrogen, in space

nuclear fusion process inside stars that joins (fuses) light nuclei together to make heavier nuclei and give out energy

nucleus particle, or particles, at the center of an atom. The plural of nucleus is nuclei.

planetesimal small body that joins together with other planetesimals to form a protoplanet and then a planet

prominence tongue of gas curling out into space above the Sun

protoplanet body about the same size as the Moon that grows by attracting more gas and dust until it becomes a planet

solar eclipse event that occurs when the Moon passes between the Sun and Earth, casting a shadow on the Earth

solar nebula cloud of gas and dust that formed the solar system

solar wind constant stream of particles flying out of the Sun in all directions

Index